Lead Like a Lion

Abdi Osman Jama, Jaak Treiman,
Liisa Välikangas, PH.D.

Copyright © 2013 Abdi Osman Jama, Jaak Treiman, Liisa Välikangas PhD

All rights reserved.

ISBN: 1511814802
ISBN-13: 978-1511814805

	Introduction	6
	The Organization of the Book	7
1	A Donkey's Brain	9
2	Into the Lion's Den	13
3	Herding Camels	15
4	The Lion, the Rat and the Zookeeper	19
5	The Drought	21
6	Misunderstood Alarm	24
7	Friendship and Thievery	26
8	The Inheritance	29
9	The Old Goat	32
10	As You Do To Others	34
11	Tails in the Ground	38
12	Who Does Not Know the Lion	40
13	Joint Ownership of a Sheep	42
	The World Changes, The Stories Remain	
	About Lions	
	About The Author	

INTRODUCTION

Can stories about a lion provide inspiration for leadership? We believe so. In this book, stories about a lion, fox, sheep, cows, and hyenas with occasional giraffes are told to teach us about the behavior of leaders and those who follow the leaders. Leaders may behave badly, indeed very badly, abuse their power and act without any concern for those who depend on the leader. These stories of betrayal of trust, manifestation of greed, and actions in flagrant self-interest are reminders of the grave responsibilities of leadership. They are warnings of the traps of leadership and the persuasions of naked power. Societies have long worked to develop rules of behavior that prevent such fall-out. Yet as these stories collected in East-Africa remind us, there is still a long way to go before we can trust leaders to behave in a civilized manner. Indeed, perhaps we need to know these stories to prevent our leaders from falling into the destructive temptation of acting out their raw impulses.

THE ORGANIZATION OF THE BOOK

Each story is first told as a parable of leadership behavior. Most stories express the dangers of unmitigated use of power. Like old children's stories, they are warnings to heed rather than examples to follow. Lions, foxes, sheep, cows, hyenas play the roles. Their concerns are common to us humans: feeding oneself, tending property, developing (and betraying) trust, making just (or unjust) decisions, giving orders to those who are in a less powerful position and depend on the powerful.

After each story is told, a discussion on the leadership lessons follow. The reader is advised to draw his or her own conclusions, of course, and heed the warnings of the story. The stories have some humor too, so we may occasionally laugh at ourselves.

Animal stories are an age-old way of communicating wisdom. We recognize ourselves and our communities in these stories. What role do you play? How do you behave as a lion-leader or as a fox-follower? Here we go. This is the first story. Sit down, and listen. You will have a chance to write your own interpretation down, too.

1 A DONKEY'S BRAIN

The lion's kingdom embraces the jungles, the forests, the grasslands and the waterways of East Africa. All are part of his kingdom. There, he is all-powerful – the supreme ruler. But, even supreme rulers get sick. The lion was sick. He was very, very sick. He could hardly lift his head. His mane was disheveled. His bones ached. His eyes watered. The lion was sure he was dying. He had tried every medicine he could think of. His illness continued to get worse. Desperate, he ordered all of the animals in his kingdom to his bedside. He asked each, in turn, to cure him. The elephant gave the lion peanut butter toast, but that didn't help. The leopard served him dung beetle pie, but that didn't help. The aardvark made a pot of insect stew, but that didn't help. The rhinoceros offered bark from the sausage tree, but that didn't help. In fact, now not only was the lion's head heavy, mane disheveled, bones aching and eyes watery, his stomach made sounds he had never heard. Finally, it was the fox's turn to try and cure lion's illness. Through hazy eyes the lion looked at the fox and gasped, "Fox. You are known for your intelligence. What should I do?" The fox answered, "You need to eat the brain of a donkey." The lion replied, "I am too weak to hunt. I don't have the strength to catch a donkey." Then, mustering all of his strength, he issued a royal command, "Fox! Bring me a donkey brain." The fox thought for a minute and then agreed to do as the lion commanded. "But," he told the lion, "I am no match for the donkey so I can't bring you just his brain. I will have the donkey come to you." "However," she continued, "Unless you issue a proclamation I won't be able to convince the donkey to come to your den. The proclamation has to announce that because you are so sick and about to die, you have decided to pass your crown on to the donkey." Sick as he was, the lion immediately snorted, "I can't make such an announcement. It's too risky to make such promises." The fox grinned and asked the lion what he was afraid of. "You're going to eat the donkey's brains anyway." The lion understood, issued the proclamation and told the fox to be on his way and to return with a donkey. The fox left. Before long, he found a donkey. The fox told the donkey that the king was very sick, would die soon and had decided to immediately pass on his crown to the donkey.

The donkey hesitated. He was reluctant to walk into the lion's den. He had heard about the proclamation but he was still scared. Finally, his desire for the crown overcame his fear. So, with his knees knocking against each other and his body shaking, the donkey and the fox walked into the lion's den. The fox told the donkey to kneel and lower his head so the lion could place his crown on donkey's head. Donkey did so but when he felt the lion's claws on his head, he ran away in a panic. The king told the fox to bring him back. The fox said she would. She found the donkey hiding in a berry patch and said, "Donkey, you and you alone were chosen to receive the lion's crown. Now you are acting like a coward. I persuaded the king to give you a second chance, but you must show him you are brave. Even if the lion's claws scratch you, you have to show the king how brave you are. If you show the slightest fear he will change his mind and not pass his crown on to you." With renewed determination the donkey responded, "Fox, I really want be king. Let's go and get the kingship." The fox and the donkey returned to the lion's den. The donkey lowered his head. Immediately, the lion broke donkey's head into two and reached in to get donkey's brain. There was no brain! Astonished, the lion asked the fox, "Where is the donkey's brain?" The fox looked matter-of-factly at the lion. "What did you expect? If he had a brain, why would he come back?"

LEADERSHIP LESSONS

A modern interpretation of this story could be a warning not to use too many consultants or at least to not let consultants run your company. There is a story similar to this one where a consultant is hired to cure a sick goat. After many potions are applied, the goat dies. As the goat's owner laments the death of his animal, the consultant retorts, "Too bad. I still had so many other cures left." According to this interpretation of the story, it is important for a leader to know the organization and be in charge of the cures that are applied. Another interpretation is to consider the story from the donkey's point of view. Do not act against your better judgment even if the possible gains are very tempting, such as someone giving you a kingdom. If it is too good to be true, it probably is! Certainly, if by chance you managed to survive the first time, do not make the same mistake again. A big difference between a wise and not-so-wise person is that a wise person doesn't repeat mistakes.

Write your own interpretation. What is the meaning of the story for you? How will it impact your leadership?

2 INTO THE LION'S DEN

It was a warm, lazy, summer afternoon. A few white, cottony clouds drifted across a bright, azure sky. Even the crickets had stopped chattering. The lion basked in the sunshine of his East African kingdom, his eyelids drooping. Rumbles from his stomach interrupted Lion's reverie. He was hungry but the day was too perfect to spend hunting. Lion did what any monarch would do. He ambled into his den and issued a royal decree ordering each of his subjects to appear before him. As always, his order was not questioned and the animals obeyed. They came, one by one: the ostrich, the camel, the donkey, the gazelle, the giraffe and all the rest. Each entered the lion's den and appeared before the lion. Finally, it was fox's turn to enter and make her appearance. She paused at the den's entrance and then, refused to enter! The lion roared in anger. "How dare you disobey my command?" But, the fox continued to refuse to enter the den. "I don't see any tracks leading away from your den, only entering," she pointed out to the lion. There was silence; then a satisfied burp echoed from the den.

Fox left and nothing more was said.

LEADERSHIP LESSONS

The ancient Greek slave Aesop may have first told a variation of this story. The leader is lazy and isn't willing to work for his rewards. Perhaps the first lesson is for followers not to obey a leader who clearly does not earn his keep. Another lesson is that followers need to pay attention to what they are asked to do. The fox escapes the fate of his compatriots by being observant. Of course, sometimes the thing that is most obvious is the hardest to notice or articulate.

Write your own interpretation. What is the meaning of the story for you? How will it impact your leadership?

3 HERDING CAMELS

The lion kept a herd of camels and used his subjects to tend them. One day it was the fox's and the ostrich's turn to tend the camels. Neither had eaten breakfast that morning and by the middle of the day both were very hungry. Fox volunteered to go into the bush and find some edible gums while the ostrich looked after the camels. Ostrich thought that was a fine idea so fox left the camels, went into the bush and found some delicious gums all of which she immediately ate. Before returning to ostrich and the camels, fox found three stones and coated each with gum so they looked like white gumballs. She brought the three white stones to the ostrich. Fox told the ostrich how lucky she had been to find good gum and offered ostrich the three white stones as her portion. By this time ostrich was starving. She took the first white stone and tried to gulp it down. It stuck in ostrich's throat.

Fox told ostrich to swallow the second white stone. "This second one will dislodge the first gumball and you will swallow both," predicted fox. Ostrich did so but the second stone stuck on top of the first one. Fox then said, "Don't worry. Swallow the third gumball. It will dislodge the first two." Ostrich did so but the third one stuck on top of the first two stones. As the day went on ostrich grew weaker and weaker and was unable to speak. When fox and ostrich returned the camels to the lion's ranch, lion met them and asked them how their day went. Fox replied that everything went very well except half way through the day ostrich became very smug and refused to speak. Hearing that, lion was disappointed and called the ostrich to him. He asked ostrich what the problem was but because of the stones queued in his throat ostrich could only reply "urkkk yackkk." The lion repeated his question. Ostrich gurgled, "urkkk yackkk." A very irritated Lion said, "Ostrich. You have one last chance to explain yourself." In desperation, ostrich looked with pleading eyes on lion and gurgled "urkkk yackkk." Now in full temper, lion leaped on the ostrich and broke its neck.

He then told fox to find someone else to help herd his camels. The next day, fox and giraffe tended the camels. At midday both were hungry. Fox volunteered to go into the bush and find some edible gums while the giraffe looked after the camels. Giraffe thought that was a fine idea so fox went into the bush and found some delicious gums. She ate all of them. Afterward, she found three stones and coated the stones with gum so they looked like white gumballs. Fox brought the three white stones to the giraffe. She told the giraffe how lucky she had been to find good gum and offered giraffe the three white stones.

Giraffe was hungry, took the first white stone and gulped it down. It lodged in giraffe's throat. "This second one will dislodge the first gumball and you will swallow both," predicted fox. Giraffe did so but the second stone stuck on top of the first one. Fox then said, "Don't worry. Swallow the third gumball. It will dislodge the first two." Giraffe did so but the third one stuck on top of the first two stones. As the day went on Giraffe grew weaker and weaker and was unable to speak. When fox and giraffe returned the camels to the lion's ranch, lion met them and asked them how their day went. Fox replied that everything went very well but half way through the day giraffe became very smug and refused to speak. Hearing that, lion was disappointed and called the giraffe to him. He asked giraffe what the problem was but because of the stones queued in his throat giraffe could only reply "urkkk yackkk." The lion repeated his question. Giraffe gurgled, "urkkk yackkk." A very irritated Lion said, "Giraffe. You have one last chance to explain yourself." In desperation, giraffe looked with pleading eyes on lion and gurgled "urkkk yackkk." Now in full temper, lion leaped on the giraffe and broke its neck.

He then told fox to find someone else to help her herd his camels. The next day, fox and aardvark went out to herd the camels. At midday both were hungry. Well, you know the story. Fox went looking for gum and brought back stones coated with gum that lodged in aardvark's throat so he could not speak. The lion killed aardvark as he had done ostrich and giraffe. Finally, there was no one left to help fox herd the camels except lion himself. The next day, early in the morning before lion and fox took the camels for the day's pasture, fox dug a deep hole, built a fire in the bottom and then covered the hole with a beautiful blanket. When she and the lion arrived near the hole, fox told lion, "You have so many things to worry about in ruling your kingdom, you must be tired. Lie down on that beautiful blanket and rest while I look after the camels." The lion did so, and the rest is history.

LEADERSHIP LESSONS

This is a cruel story where the clever guy repeatedly takes advantage of the kinder fellows. Sadly, the good guys lose. The lesson may be not to take anything for granted, especially from someone with a questionable reputation. Also, the leader too easily trusted, and was eventually betrayed by someone who made his life easy. The leadership lesson is about the necessity to work hard and not simply take the easy way out offered by someone who eventually will take advantage of your indolence.

Write your own interpretation. What is the meaning of the story for you? How will it impact your leadership?

4 THE LION, THE RAT AND THE ZOOKEEPER

Once upon a time a rat had the misfortune to be snared by the lion. The rat begged the lion not to kill him. "I promise that if you free me I will, someday, help you." The king of the jungle snickered. Then, the more he thought about how silly the idea was of a rat helping him, he began to chuckle, and then laugh uproariously. As he caught his breath between fits of laughter, lion managed to ask the rat, "How can you, a little runt, ever help me?" The rat replied, "Life is not always what you expect. Appearances can be deceiving." The lion, shaking his head but feeling magnanimous, let the rat go.

Two years later, the lion was hunting in the bush. Unbeknownst to him a zookeeper was in the area, capturing animals for his zoo. Carelessly, lion stepped on a net that immediately wrapped itself around him, lifted him high and left him hanging from a tree branch. The rat saw the king of the jungle, wrapped in a net, swinging from a high tree branch. Quickly, the rat scurried up the tree and began chewing the net's strands, one by one. Rat could hear the approaching zookeeper's trucks, filled with empty cages, rattling in the distance. Lion pleaded with the rat, "Hurry. Hurry. Please hurry." Finally, as the sound of the rattling cages grew louder and louder, rat finished chewing the last strand that trapped the lion in the net. The lion leapt to the ground and quickly ran into the bush. Only then did the lion pause and realize the truth of what rat had said two years earlier. Lion promised himself never again to judge anyone by their size or appearance.

LEADERSHIP LESSONS

This is a beautiful story that points out how everyone, no matter how small or insignificant, is important. It is also a tribute to one's word – keeping promises. While in this story it is a leader who is learning the lesson, the same applies to all of us. Never hesitate to help someone in need; you may need their help in return one day. It is much better to have friends who owe you than enemies whom you left dying and who will attempt a pay back one day. That way you can sleep in peace, and should one day you be in trouble, trust in getting help from someone whom you helped first.

Write your own interpretation. What is the meaning of the story for you? How will it impact your leadership?

5 THE DROUGHT

Somalia was devastated. Rainless for over two years, the grass was brown, the trees wilted and all the animals were starving. Lion had convened conference after conference of experts hoping for guidance in surviving the drought. Finally, with almost no food left in their reserves, lion decreed that if any hunter were successful, the hunter's catch would be shared as he dictated. As supreme ruler, he would decide in his sole and absolute discretion, how all food would be divided. Anyone objecting to the lion's decision would be immediately and severely punished. After many more days of continued starvation, hyena, who opposed lion's dictatorship, returned to the lion's court with a successful kill. Lion called an assembly to decide how to share the meat among the hungry beasts. Lion, not knowing what to say, talked and talked and talked – and said nothing.

Finally, in desperation, he said, "I need somebody to honestly distribute the meat among my starving subjects." Everyone was silent. Each was afraid that if they volunteered for the task, lion would not like how they divided the food and would punish them. Finally lion turned to fox and asked her to distribute the food. Lion looked around and asked if anyone disagreed with his choice. Everyone replied, "Yes sir. Fox is an excellent choice." Fox slowly moved towards the meat and started this conversation with lion: Miss Fox: "Divide the meat into two halves." The lion roared his approval. Miss fox: "One half goes to lion." The lion roared his approval. Miss Fox: "Divide the remaining half by two." The lion roared his approval. Miss Fox: "One half of that goes to lion." The lion roared his approval while the rest of the beasts looked on, angry but helpless. Miss Fox: "Divide the remaining half by two." The lion roared his approval. Miss Fox: "One half of that goes to lion." The lion roared his approval. The fox kept dividing each remaining half of the meat in the same manner until all but one small bite had been allocated to the lion. Miss Fox: This very small, bite size piece goes to me!"

Lion: "Miss Fox who taught you to judge this way?" Fox: "Hyena's eye!"

The rest of the beasts stalked away hungry and angry. When the drought ended they rebelled against lion's dictatorship and toppled it.

LEADERSHIP LESSONS

Here we have a story within a story. The story of the "hyena's eye" goes like this: Once, a lion, a hyena and a fox went hunting. They caught a sheep. The lion said the sheep had to be divided. The hyena said he would take the back parts, the lion the front parts and the fox could have the feet and entrails. Hearing this, the displeased lion struck the hyena on the head so hard that one of hyena's eyes fell out. Then the lion told the fox to make the division. The fox took the head, the intestines and the feet for himself and the hyena and gave the rest to the lion. Pleased, the lion asked the fox who taught him to judge so well. The fox replied, "The hyena's eye."

The fox, remembering what happened to the hyena when the hyena didn't please the lion, divides the only available food so the lion gets almost all of it. This increases everyone's resentment against the lion. When things get better the resentment doesn't disappear. Instead, better times present an opportunity to topple the ruler. People have not forgotten their merciless treatment and the earlier lack of concern for their needs. As a leader, do not build resentment toward you that waits and simmers until there is a good time to rebel. Show mercy and justice even if it means smaller portions on which to feed one's ego.

Write your own interpretation. What is the meaning of the story for you? How will it impact your leadership?

6 MISUNDERSTOOD ALARM

Once upon a time there was a large farm. On that farm a chicken and a donkey were eating peacefully. A lion passed by the farm, looked at the donkey and saw a meal. The chicken saw the lion move stealthily toward the donkey. She began to run around, her wings flapping, her cackling louder than a cacophony of hail hitting a tin roof. The lion fled, convinced the farmer had seen him and that he would be shot at any moment. When the donkey saw the lion run away, he was sure there was something very dangerous out there. "Why else would the king of the jungle run so scared?" So, braying "Danger, danger" the donkey followed the lion. The lion heard the donkey galloping behind him, stopped, turned around, killed it and enjoyed his meal.

LEADERSHIP LESSONS

This is a story of the use of smart strategy that benefits from serendipity. The leader takes advantage of a situation that was somewhat accidental, outside his or her intention. Yet the opportunity arises, and the leader acts. While acting with care, another situation emerges that requires quick decision-making and fast action.

Write your own interpretation. What is the meaning of the story for you? How will it impact your leadership?

7 FRIENDSHIP AND THIEVERY

The lion and fox were friends. They were also thieves. One day as they roamed near the headwaters of the Shebelle River they saw, on the other side, a farm rich in crops and animals. They decided to cross the river and see what they could steal from the farm. The lion, being a strong swimmer, told the fox to get on his back in order to cross the river. Once on the river's other side they stalked the farm. They saw some fat chickens to their liking, caught them, put them in sacks and carried them to a nearby meadow. They proceeded to eat them. The fox ate her chickens quickly and with her smaller stomach was soon full. When she finished her lunch, she told the lion, who had not yet come close to filling his stomach, "After I finish lunch I always sing." The lion, still trying to finish his meal, begged the fox, "Don't sing. The farmer will hear you and come after us. First, let me finish my lunch." Fox ignored him and started to sing. The farmer heard the singing and came running with a shotgun and an axe. The fox fled. The farmer wounded the lion with his axe but the wounded lion still managed to escape.

When the lion reached the river, fox was waiting. She did not know how to swim. The fox asked the lion, "Can I cross the river on your back?" The lion agreed and fox jumped on the lion's back. When they arrived at the middle of the river, where it is very deep, he told the fox, "After I have eaten my lunch I always take a bath." The fox begged, "No! No! Please don't take a bath. I will drown." "I am sorry," replied the lion, "but I always take a bath after lunch." Slowly he let his backbone sink below the waterline. "Help!" shouted the fox. The lion looked at her and asked, "Are you sorry for what you did." "Yes," replied the fox with all the sincerity he could muster while gagging on river water. The lion felt sorry for the fox and told her he couldn't let her die. He finished crossing the river with fox again on his back. When they reached the riverbank the fox and lion both promised they would never put the other in danger again. "But," reminded the lion, "what I did was tit-for-tat." They both laughed.

LEADERSHIP LESSONS

This story has nice humor to it – being able to laugh together is an important sign of friendship. The tit-for-tat strategy is well known for efficiently discouraging opportunism. If I expect to be treated like I treat others, it is wise to behave well toward others. The lion also wanted to teach a lesson to the selfish fox. The lesson was well taught – no one died yet the fox was scared enough to probably remember the lesson. Laughing together afterwards confirmed that the two were still friends.

Write your own interpretation. What is the meaning of the story for you? How will it impact your leadership?

8 THE INHERITANCE

Once upon a time, there was a fox and a hyena. They had known each other since childhood. When they grew up, hyena was wealthy and owned hundreds of sheep. Fox owned only a few sheep. Fox was jealous and wanted to improve her holdings. Hyena had always been impressed by how clever the fox was. He thought he could learn cleverness from her. They saw more and more of each other until one day Hyena proposed marriage. Fox accepted. Some weeks after their marriage, fox heard that lion had been looking for someone to care for his sheep. Fox went to the lion and asked if the position was still vacant. Lion said it was – he was still looking for a sheepherder. He had other things to do besides looking after sheep. Fox sympathized with the lion about how hard it was to find good help. She then slyly suggested to lion, "You must be tired, looking after all those sheep for so long. Why don't you go to sleep and I'll look after them."

The lion liked the suggestion but he warned her to

be very alert. He didn't want thieves stealing his sheep. Fox told lion not to worry. Lion then went into his den to sleep. While the lion slept fox ate the biggest and fattest sheep. She ate everything except a small, bloody piece of meat that she took to the sleeping hyena and rubbed over his mouth. When the lion woke he counted his sheep but found the best one was missing. He asked the fox, "Where is that sheep?" The fox said, my husband, the hyena, ate the sheep. When I tried to stop him he slammed my face to the ground. The lion ran to the hyena and found him sleeping, his mouth covered with blood. The lion immediately killed the hyena, convinced that hyena had eaten his sheep. Fox then inherited all of hyenas' sheep.

LEADERSHIP LESSONS

This is a story of betrayal. While the fox ends up inheriting the hyena's sheep, the deeds are not worthy of a leader. Perhaps the story can be read as a warning: be careful whom you trust, especially if it is their cleverness you admire. It is important to keep one's distance long enough to learn to know someone well enough to be able to trust them. Of course, trust invites betrayal, and one way to interpret the story might be to show compassion to those who have trusted, in good faith, and yet have been betrayed. This story also reminds a leader not to be asleep while leading. It is the leader's responsibility to know what is going on in the organization. Do not take anybody else's word for it, in particular, if they have a reason to lie for gain.

Write your own interpretation. What is the meaning of the story for you? How will it impact your leadership?

9 THE OLD GOAT

Every night lion and hyena hunted for food. They searched the forests, avoiding quicksand, Black Mamba and Boomslang vipers and hunters. Sometimes they were successful, sometimes not. They decided their lives would be much easier if they had their own sheep ranch. "But," lion asked, "Where will we get the sheep?" Hyena suggested that one night, instead of doing their usual hunting, they should find a sheep ranch and take some of the sheep to their own place. "We can keep them and whenever we are hungry, our meal will be right there." Lion wondered how they could keep the sheep safe from thieves and other animals looking for a meal. Hyena responded, "Our ranch will be prestigious. You are king of the jungle. No one will dare come close. And, it will be well guarded. We will also brand the sheep so if anyone does steal one, everyone will know it has been stolen." Lion was convinced and lion and hyena went looking for sheep to steal.

They found a large sheep ranch but it was so

strongly protected that lion and hyena were both afraid to enter and steal the sheep. Fortunately, nearby they saw an old goat. They decided to take the goat, as that was better than nothing. Lion ordered hyena to carry the goat, which was much heavier than it looked. Hyena carried the goat for three nights and three days. When they finally arrived back at their place they were very tired and very hungry, especially the hyena. Lion told hyena, "I will now eat the goat. Please leave. I prefer to eat alone." Hyena implored the lion to give him something. "Please give me something. Even just the tail will do." The lion replied, "Not this time." He then ate the entire goat by himself.

LEADERSHIP LESSONS

Greed is universal. This story warns of how power corrupts – how easy it is to forget your friends when you have power and they cannot instantly retaliate. From those who have very little, it is said, the rest is taken away too. Or, in modern language, the winner takes it all, including the tail. This kind of behavior is not leadership – it is greed. A leader must always be just rewarding hard work and accomplishments. Do not become a parasitic ruler.

Write your own interpretation. What is the meaning of the story for you? How will it impact your leadership?

10 AS YOU DO TO OTHERS

Once upon a time there was a wide meadow, lush with grass. The meadow was home to three cows. One cow was brown, one was black and the third cow was white. The meadow's four pigeon wood trees provided noontime shade and a little creek meandered through the lush grass, providing fresh water. The three cows were happy. They were best friends. They liked their meadow and each other and most of the time browsed together. One day a lion came to the meadow and saw the three cows grazing. He thought to himself, "This is a good place. I can stay here and hunt the cows.

They can provide me food for a long time." The next day lion went to hunt. He saw the white cow napping a little distance from her friends. He sprung at her. But, the black and the brown cows warned their white friend and came to help their friend. During the fierce battle the lion was injured and barely escaped with his life. "Oh, that was not easy. I was almost killed by those cows. I cannot get even a bit of food while those cows are together. I must do something about it," thought the lion. The next day the lion went to the cows. "Please listen to me. Yesterday I wanted to talk to the white cow and she thought I was going to attack her. Then all of you attacked and nearly killed me. I came here in peace." "You wanted to attack me while I was asleep. You are la liar. We don't believe you," said the white cow. "No. I wasn't going to attack you. I wanted to talk." "So what do you want to say?" said the brown cow. "When I saw this meadow for the first time, I liked it. I just wanted to ask you if you would let me stay here and in return I will protect you against your enemies." The cows talked to each other and after much consideration, said, "Ok, You can stay here. But, don't come close to us. We will let you stay here and you will have to protect us." "Thank you and don't be afraid of me. I can hunt small animals and I will never harm you," said the lion.

So the lion stayed in the meadow for ten days. On the tenth day he saw that the white cow was grazing at the other end of the meadow from the black and brown cows and was separated from them by the pigeon trees. Lion went to the two cows and said, "You know, I think this place is very nice but it won't stay that way if your fat, white friend keeps eating the nice grasses. She eats a lot more than either of you. And, she is a different color. We are dark and she is white. Let me kill her so there will be enough grass for both of you." After some discussion the two cows agreed that the lion could kill their friend, which the lion promptly did. He ate his meat and had food for quite a time.

Two weeks later lion saw that the black cow and brown cow were browsing separately. He went to the brown cow and said, "I want to be your best friend but first you have to prove your friendship."

"How can I prove it?" said the brown cow. "Well, I have thought about that for quite a while. You and I are very similar. We are the same color. Let me kill the black cow so this wonderful meadow will be only for brown cows." The brown cow agreed and the lion attacked and killed the black cow. Lion was content for sometime. Then he became hungry again. He went to the brown cow and said, "You are my best friend and of course I am your best friend. Now your best friend is hungry and there is no meat except your meat. Get ready to be killed for I am too hungry and cannot wait. The brown cow said to the lion, "Why do you want to eat me after I did all those favors for you? " The lion replied, when you agreed that I could eat your friends you gave me permission to kill and eat you.

LEADERSHIP LESSONS

This is a powerful story. It teaches us a lesson not only of being true and not betraying one's friends but it does so in a way that underlines the importance of respecting people equally regardless of their appearance. People may look different, but they are still the same, just as you and I. The story also is reminiscent of the Finnish saying that, "If you give evil your little finger, evil will take your whole hand." Once you set yourself on the path of betrayal, it is difficult to stop. And in the end someone will hold you liable for your behavior and treat you as your treated others. You will lose everyone's respect as a leader and your followers will not heed you. You will die in shame.

Write your own interpretation. What is the meaning of the story for you? How will it impact your leadership?

11 TAILS IN THE GROUND

Each day was the same. Whether the landscape was drenched in sunshine or a downpour, lion would wake up, stretch, groom his mane, drink some water from the nearby river and then hunt for his meal. Sometimes he would find his meal early in the day; sometimes it took all day; sometimes he would find nothing. Then, Lion had an inspiration! He would capture and pen a flock of sheep. No longer would he have to hunt every day. He would have time for his other duties. But, who would look after his flock while he performed his other duties? Lion thought about it and decided to ask fox to be his sheepherder. Fox agreed.

Every day lion would come to where the sheep were grazing, pick one out, and dine on mutton. Fox watched and decided he could do the same. Every day, after the lion had his meal and left, fox would pick out a sheep and have her meal. When she finished, she took the sheep's tail and stuck it into the ground. One day the lion looked at the dwindling herd and asked the fox why there were so few sheep left. He told the fox, "I had thirty sheep. I have had this herd for only ten days. I have eaten only one sheep each day but now there are only ten sheep left. What has happened to the other ten?" Fox told the lion, "This place has such soft sand that the sheep sink into it and only their tails remain visible." Fox then showed lion the tails. The lion pulled on the tails, trying to get the sheep out. Each time, he only got the tail. Frustrated, the lion told fox, "This is not a good place for sheep. Let's find something better."

LEADERSHIP LESSONS

This story is quite humorous in its cleverness. The fox comes up with an explanation that, on its face, is believable, yet untrue. There are at least two leadership lessons: Be aware enough to distinguish fanciful yet true explanations of events from those that are cover-ups. And, think of your followers, not just yourself. What will they eat?

Write your own interpretation. What is the meaning of the story for you? How will it impact your leadership?

12 WHO DOES NOT KNOW THE LION

A lion steals a sheep and runs away. The owner of the sheep considers his options. It is dangerous to go after a lion. But the owner has never met a lion, and thus does not know what kind of a dangerous beast it is. He therefore runs after his sheep, and by luck perhaps, gets his sheep back. Only the person who does not know the lion can get his sheep back.

LEADERSHIP LESSONS

This short, beautiful story is about the role knowledge plays in our lives. Going after a lion to get one's sheep back requires true courage, but if you do not know what kind of a beast a lion is, perhaps out of mere ignorance, you will chase the lion. Sometimes great deeds are accomplished because one does not know any better. For example, one may not know or may not correctly assess the odds of failure. At other times great innovations are achieved because one does not know that most experts consider the attempted activity impossible to accomplish. In those cases ignorance plays a productive role in our lives. Sometimes a leader must allow and even cultivate such entrepreneurship: the persistent effort to accomplish something quite unlikely to succeed. When it occasionally does, the pay-off is great!

Write your own interpretation. What is the meaning of the story for you? How will it impact your leadership?

13 JOINT OWNERSHIP OF A SHEEP

Once upon a time a lion and a fox went hunting together. They saw a sheep. The fox chased the sheep into a box canyon where the sheep squeezed passed huge boulders, into a cave. The lion, using his strength, moved the boulders and the sheep was trapped. Lion and fox, while celebrating their success, agreed they would keep the live sheep as a reminder of their joint effort. They promised each other that they would never, ever eat the sheep.

Some time later there was a severe drought. Food was scarce and fox and lion were very hungry. Fox asked the lion to end their agreement. Lion refused. The hungry, disgruntled fox then walked into some nearby brush. She came back with her face and head oiled. The lion asked, "How did you get all that oil on your face and head?" The fox replied, "I wasn't paying attention and bumped into a tree. The tree released oil, which I then used to cream myself." The lion, thinking the oil might taste good and if not, would at least make him look more handsome, saw a tree. With his head down he ran at full speed and rammed the tree. The impact killed him. Fox then ate the sheep.

LEADERSHIP LESSONS

Being vain may cost one's life. The fox again shows how strategy overcomes might by appealing to someone's weaknesses. Turning a light, accidental head-on with a tree into a strategic weapon is quite skillful though merciless. Hunger seems to prevail over other considerations. A leader should remember that people in dire need become desperate and potentially determined.
Write your own interpretation. What is the meaning of the story for you? How will it impact your leadership?

THE WORLD CHANGES, THE STORIES REMAIN

Myths are everywhere. A famous anthropologist Joseph Campbell studied universal mythology (see for example his book titled The Hero With a Thousand Faces); Rudyard Kipling wrote about powerful stories of the jungle. The Panchatantra, a collection of ancient animal fables from India written in sanksrit, was arguably intended as instruction in political science. Another old collection of stories, Aesop's Fables, is credited to a slave called Aesop who is believed to have lived in ancient Greece. These fables are often told to children as moral education. Throughout history animals have played an important role in literature and in culture. Animal stories have been used to help explain how the world and society were formed. Sometimes they are used to teach a lesson. Mythological animals can be common animals such as frogs or bears, but they can also be animal-like supernatural creatures that never existed in the real world.

Many animal stories are stories with a moral lesson; they are survival guides or how guides as to how to live our lives. In such stories animals usually have human traits, they can speak and they posses human-like qualities. For example, in one of Aesop's fables, The Fox and the Grapes, the fox tries to reach a bunch of hanging grapes. When his repeated attempts are unsuccessful, he says, "I am sure they are sour, anyway." One interpretation of the story's moral lesson is that it is easy to despise what you cannot get. Many still famous, common sayings come from these old stories. Animal stories have also been used to explain and even criticize society. For example, one of the most famous animal stories that address societal issues is George Orwell's Animal Farm.

It is a story of exploited farm animals that revolt against the farmer and take over the farm. The story has a message about world politics and the animal's actions can be seen as a metaphor for the Russian revolution and its aftermath. Here again, the animals have human characteristics so it is easy to identify with them. We all draw our own lessons from these stories that the human kind has told each other for thousands of years. While the lessons and the reader's or listener's ability to learn may vary greatly, the stories remain. Perhaps we still have a lot to learn from them!

ABOUT LIONS

The lion is a symbol of power, courage, strength and wealth. It has been depicted in sculptures, in paintings, on national flags, and in contemporary films and literature. It appears on the Finnish and Estonian coat-of-arms, two geographic areas where the lion has not been found for at least the past 10,000 years. Certainly, the lion is a powerful, universal symbol. As such, it has been used as the centerpiece for stories rooted in the folk traditions of such geographically disparate areas as Africa, Europe, India and North America,

ABOUT THE AUTHOR

Abdi Osman Jama

Abdi Osman Jama is the CEO of ISI. He has broad experience as an entrepreneur and senior management consultant. He is former CEO of Eactels ltd, a Finnish IT company. Abdi has managed many global projects and been lecturer at Evtek University, currently Metropolia University of Applied Sciences in the computer engineering program. He has also taught Business & Technology Alignment in the Haaga-Helia executive MBA program. Abdi participates in management and leadership development discussions and been quoted in several top management and business magazines, including both Harvard Business Review and Bloomberg. He has Masters in Industrial Management from Helsinki Metropolia University of Applied Sciences.

Jaak Treiman

Jaak Treiman is the general counsel of Innovation Democracy Inc. Jaak Treiman's undergraduate and legal education were at the University of Southern California. He also holds a Master's degree from the University of

Chicago. As an attorney, he has represented foreign commercial enterprises in their American activities and American firms engaged in overseas business. Born in Estonia, Jaak has been active in helping the Baltic states. He was Board Chair of the U.S.-Baltic Foundation while USBF administered a $2.9 million grant made by the USAID to further democratic reforms in Estonia, Latvia and Lithuania. Before the Soviet withdrawal from Estonia, he worked with Estonian dissidents. He has met with Presidents Gerald Ford, Ronald Reagan and George H. W. Bush concerning Baltic affairs. He is Estonia's Honorary Consul in California. "

Liisa Välikangas, PhD.

Liisa Välikangas is the president of Innovation Democracy Inc. her areas of interest are innovation, strategy and global change. She is a professor of innovation management at AALTO University. Her research has been published in Harvard Business Review, MIT Sloan Management Review, WallStreet Journal, among other leading journals, and presented to various academic and executive audiences. The academy of management awarded her a divisional best action research and the strategic management society has also awarded her a conference prize for integrating theory and practice. Last year she has a new book, the Resilient Organization, how adaptive cultures thrive even when strategy fails (mcgraw-hill, 2010).

www.ingramcontent.com/pod-product-compliance
Lightning Source LLC
Chambersburg PA
CBHW020711180526
45163CB00008B/3041